# Materials:
## and Their Uses

David Byrne

*Photo Credits*

Chris Honeywell, front cover, back cover, title page, contents page, pages 4, 5, 6 middle and bottom, 7, 9, 10 middle, 11, 13 main, 14 top, 15 main, 17, 19 and 20.

Trip/R. Drury, page 6 top left.

FLPA/Silvestris, page 6 top right.

George Bernard/Science Photo Library, page 10 top.

Trevor Clifford, pages 13 top and 21 bottom. Tony Stone Images/Roger Markham Smith, page 15 inset top.

Tony Stone Images/Baron Wolman, page 15 inset middle.

Panos Pictures/Neil Cooper, page 16 top.

Silvestris/Heiner Heine, page 16 middle. Trip/H. Rogers, page 16 bottom.

Zefa/CPA, page 21 top

*Illustrations*

All illustrations by Oxford Illustrators.

Discovery World:
Materials and Their Uses

©1998 Rigby
a division of Reed Elsevier Inc.
500 Coventry Lane
Crystal Lake, IL 60014

All rights reserved. No part of this publication may be reproduced or transmitted in any form by any means, electronic or mechanical, including photocopying, recording, taping, or any information storage and retrieval system without permission in writing from the publisher.

02 01 00
10 9 8 7 6 5 4

Printed in the United States of America
ISBN 0-7635-7232-2

Visit Rigby on the
World Wide Web at
http://www.rigby.com

# Contents

Types of Materials . . . . . . . . . . . . . . . . 4

Wood . . . . . . . . . . . . . . . . . . . . . . . . . . . 6

Paper . . . . . . . . . . . . . . . . . . . . . . . . . . 8

Metal . . . . . . . . . . . . . . . . . . . . . . . . . 10

Glass . . . . . . . . . . . . . . . . . . . . . . . . . 12

Plastic . . . . . . . . . . . . . . . . . . . . . . . . 14

Clay . . . . . . . . . . . . . . . . . . . . . . . . . . 16

Cement . . . . . . . . . . . . . . . . . . . . . . . 18

Save Our Resources . . . . . . . . . . . . . 20

Materials and Their Properties . . . . 22

Index . . . . . . . . . . . . . . . . . . . . . . . . 24

# Types of Materials

Wood, metal, glass, and plastic are some of the many different types of materials. The things we use every day are made from different materials.

Some materials come from trees or things under the ground. These are called natural materials. Other materials are made by people. These are called man-made materials.

# Wood

Wood is a natural material. There are two types of wood. Softwood is made from evergreen trees. Hardwood is made from trees that lose their leaves.

softwood forest

hardwood forest

Trees are cut down and cut into planks. The planks are dried. This is called seasoning.

Some wood is made from lots of very small pieces of wood pressed together. This type of wood is very hard and heavy.

## Wood

- burns
- is not magnetic 
- does not conduct electricity 
- absorbs liquid 

## Wood is used to make

- furniture
- musical instruments
- paper
- charcoal for barbecues

# Paper

Paper is a man-made material. Most paper is made from wood. The wood is broken into chips. The chips are mixed with water and chemicals to make pulp.

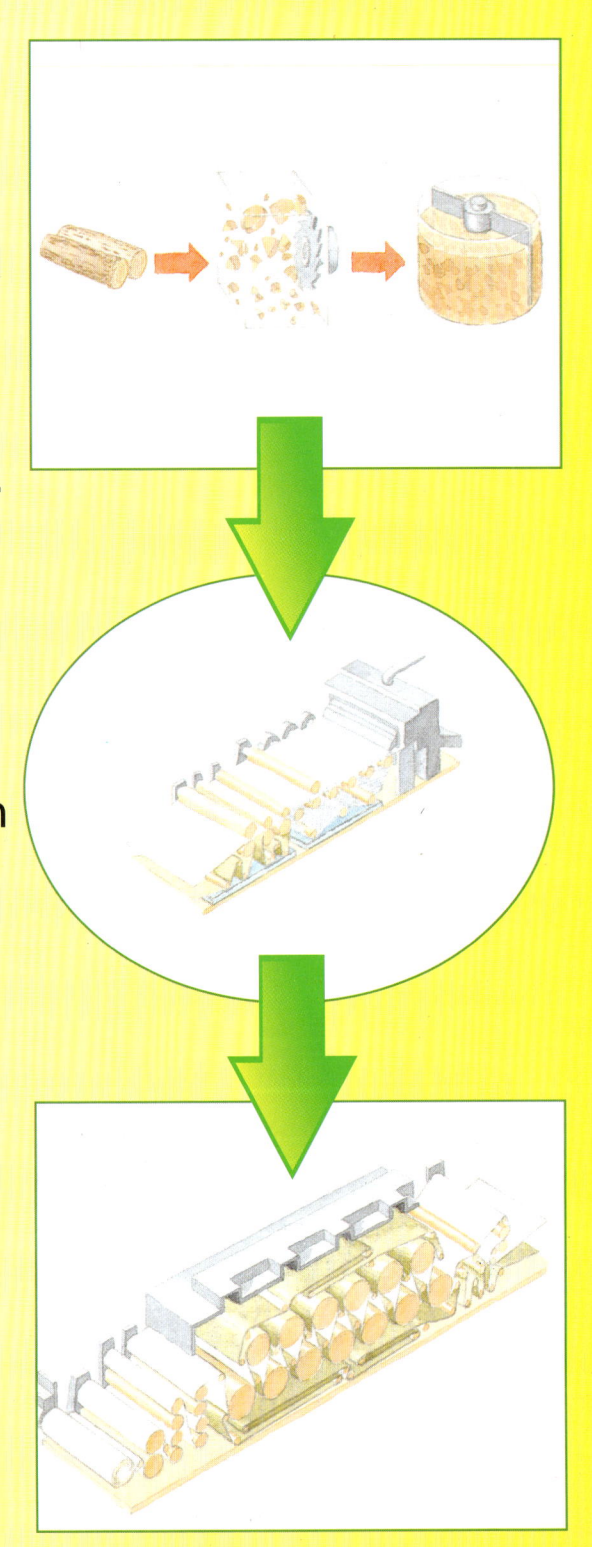

The pulp is spread onto a moving belt. The belt carries the pulp through large rollers. The rollers squeeze the water out.

Hot rollers dry the paper. The paper is made into large rolls.

## Paper

- burns
- is not magnetic
- does not conduct electricity
- absorbs liquid

## Paper is used to make

- books and newspapers
- tissues
- cards
- boxes and some candy wrappers

# Metal

gold

silver

Some metals are natural materials. These metals are found in the ground, such as gold and silver.

Some natural metals are found in rocks. The most common ones are aluminium and iron. Mines are dug to take the rocks out of the ground.

Some metals are man-made materials. These are made when natural metals are mixed together. This new metal is called an alloy.

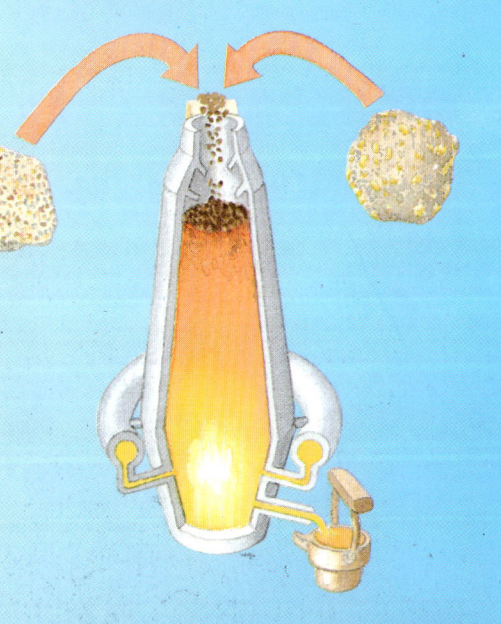

## Metal

- is usually magnetic
- usually conducts electricity
- is waterproof
- melts when it is heated

## Metal is used to make

- cans
- nails and screws
- knives, forks, and spoons
- cars and bikes

# Glass

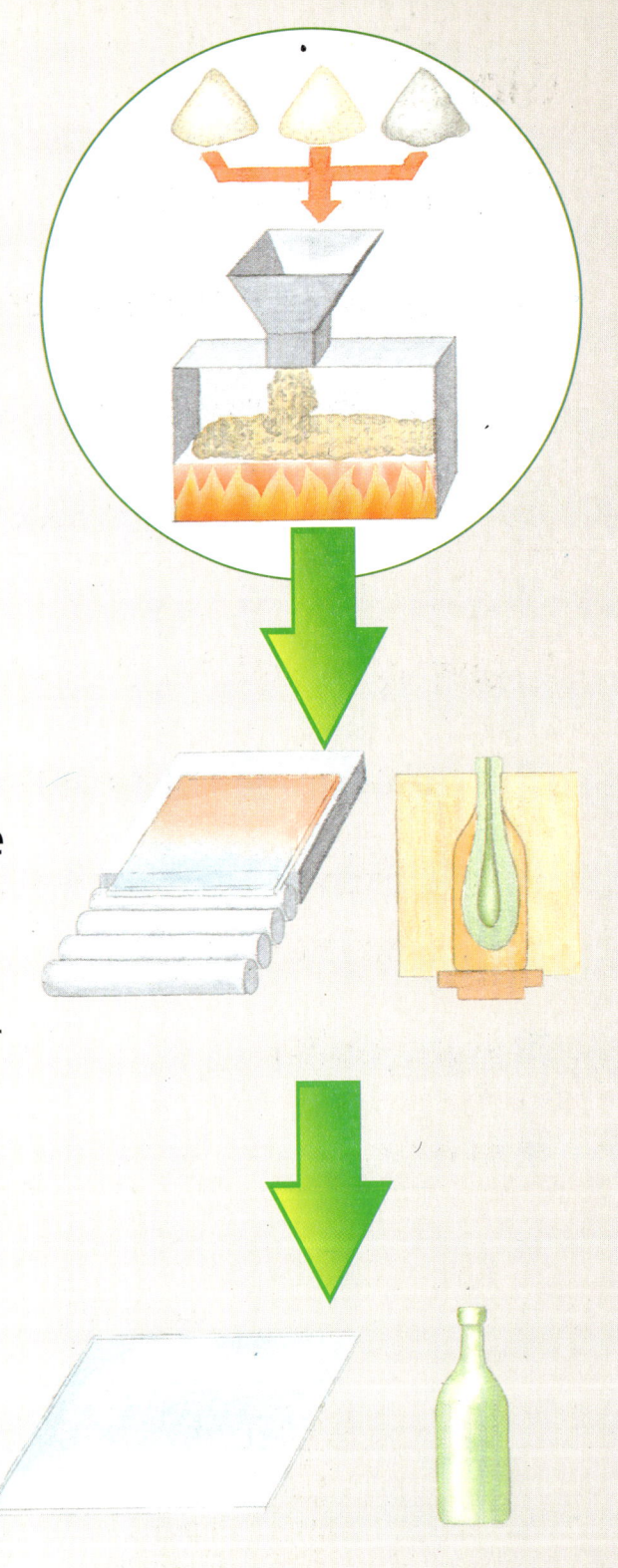

Glass is a man-made material. It is made by heating sand and chemicals together to make liquid glass.

The hot liquid glass can be made into many shapes. It can be shaped by putting it into a mold. It can be shaped by spreading it into a flat sheet.

As the glass cools, it hardens and sets.

# Glass

- is not magnetic
- is usually transparent
- is waterproof
- melts when it is heated

## Glass is used to make

- bottles and containers
- lenses in glasses, telescopes, and microscopes
- light bulbs
- windows

# Plastic

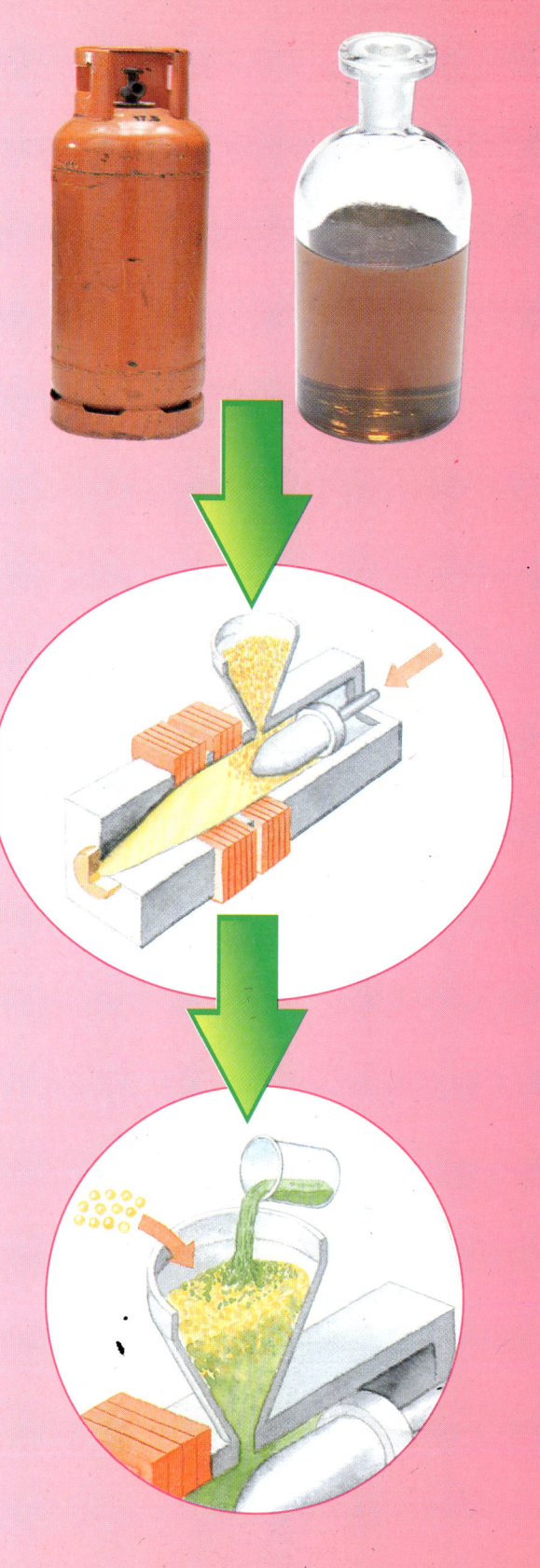

Plastic is a man-made material. It is made in a factory by heating chemicals together.

Some chemicals make soft plastic. The plastic can be made into shapes in a machine. Some chemicals make hard plastic. This can be used to make boats and aircraft.

Colored dye can be added to the chemicals.

# Plastic

- ❌ is not magnetic
- ❌ does not conduct electricity 
- 💧 is waterproof 
- 🔥 sometimes melts when it is heated

## Plastic is used to make

- containers and plastic bags
- waterproof clothes
- toys
- boats and aircraft

# Clay

Clay is a natural material. It is taken from the ground.

Clay can be made into many shapes. A potter can shape it using a special wheel.

Clay gets very hard if it is heated in a kiln or oven. This process is called firing. Clay is glazed and fired to make it strong.

# Clay

- ❌ is not magnetic
- ❌ does not conduct electricity
- absorbs liquid if it is not fired
- is waterproof if it is fired

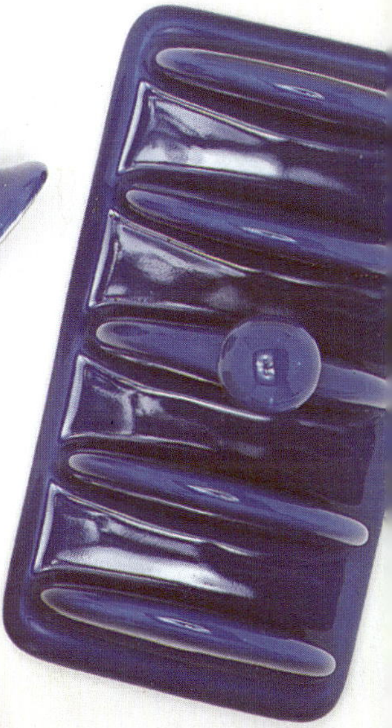

## Clay is used to make

- plates, cups, and bowls
- jewelery
- bricks
- tiles for walls and floors

# Cement

Cement is a man-made material. It is made by heating clay and chalk together.

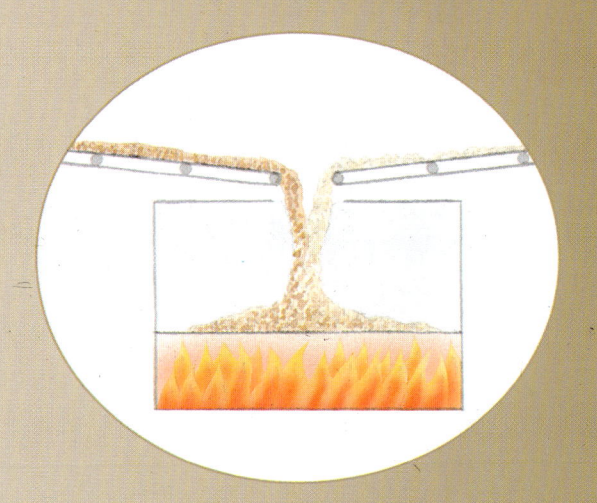

Sand, gravel, and water are mixed with cement to make concrete. Concrete is used to make sidewalks and roads.

Sand and water are mixed with cement to make mortar. Mortar holds bricks together. The bricks in houses are held together with mortar.

# Cement

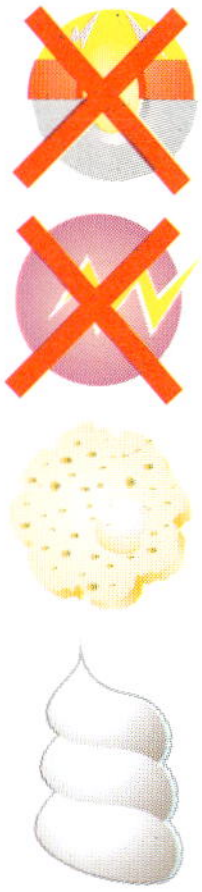

- is not magnetic
- does not conduct electricity
- absorbs liquid
- gets very hard when it is mixed with water and left to dry

## Cement is used to make

- concrete for sidewalks and roads
- mortar to hold bricks together

# Save Our Resources

Every day we throw garbage away. The garbage that we throw away can cause pollution and hurt the environment.

A lot of garbage can be used again. Aluminium and steel cans, glass bottles, plastic containers, and paper can all be recycled.

Special factories recycle different materials.

Metals are melted and used to make new cans. Glass is melted and used to make new bottles. Plastic bottles can be used to make clothes. Paper can be used to make new paper products.

You can help by collecting materials for recycling at school and at home.

# Materials and Their Properties

| Materials \ Properties | burns | magnetic | conducts electricity |
|---|---|---|---|
| wood | 🔥 | | |
| paper | 🔥 | | |
| metal | | ✓ | ⚡ |
| glass | | | |
| plastic | | | |
| clay | | | |
| cement | | | |

| transparent | absorbs liquid | waterproof | melts when heated | gets hard when mixed with water |
|---|---|---|---|---|
| | | | | |
| | | | | |
| | | | | |
| | | | | |
| | | | | |
| | | | | |
| | | | | |

# Index

a
b
c
d
e
f
g
h
i
j
k
l
m
n
o
p
q
r
s
t
u
v
w
x
y
z

alloy  10
aluminium  10, 20

cement  18–19, 22
chalk  18
chemicals  8, 12, 14
clay  16–17, 18, 22
concrete  18–19

glass  12–13, 20–21, 22
gold  10
gravel  18

hardwood  6

iron  10

metal  10–11, 21, 22
mortar  18–19

paper  7, 8–9, 20–21, 22
plastic  14–15, 20–21, 22

sand  12, 18
silver  10
softwood  6

trees  6

water  8, 18–19
wood  6–7, 8, 22